IMAGES
of England

EAST GRINSTEAD
AND ITS ENVIRONS

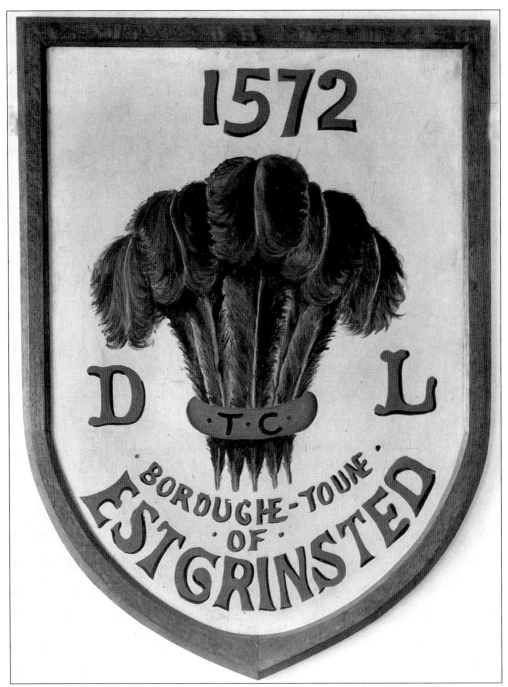

East Grinstead's seal of arms, May 1950. This is a copy painted by Frederick Hounsome (whose nephew Tony was for many years a projectionist at the town's Radio Centre cinema) and was based on a drawing in W.H. Hills's *History of East Grinstead*. The original grant of arms was drawn on parchment but disappeared some time after 1887. This copy, which measures 2ft 9in by 2ft, is now kept in the Town Museum. (Harold Connold)

IMAGES
of England

EAST GRINSTEAD
AND ITS ENVIRONS

Compiled by
David Gould

TEMPUS

First published 2001
Copyright © David Gould, 2001

Tempus Publishing Limited
The Mill, Brimscombe Port,
Stroud, Gloucestershire, GL5 2QG

ISBN 0 7524 2245 6

Typesetting and origination by
Tempus Publishing Limited
Printed in Great Britain by
Midway Colour Print, Wiltshire

Acknowledgements

Acknowledgements and thanks are tendered to the following for their assistance and the use of their copyright photographs:

East Grinstead Town Museum Trustees, *East Grinstead Courier*, *East Grinstead Observer*, N. Freeman, L.S. Laycock, M.J. Leppard, N.H. Pearson and N. Sherry. I am grateful also to K. Brown, Mrs J. Glynn, Mrs F. McElvenny, B.J. Roberts and B. Ward for certain identifications.

Contents

East Grinstead fire brigade's annual display, *c.* 1905. The location is thought to be the grounds of Imberhorne. A fireman is rescuing a dummy man from the top of the specially erected tower using a mobile extendable ladder. (Arthur Harding)

Introduction

Another book of old photographs of East Grinstead! This one, however, includes not only photographs but drawings, advertisements, programme covers and even a railway timetable. The period covered ranges from 1855, when the earliest known photographs of East Grinstead were taken, to 1990.

This compilation eschews all street scenes in which nothing is happening, for they have been well represented in both *East Grinstead* (Alan Sutton, 1995) and *Around East Grinstead* (Sutton Publishing, 1997). Therefore, taken in isolation, the present work will give an incomplete and 'unbalanced' survey of the town and its surrounding villages; there are no pictures of St Swithun's church or St Margaret's Convent. For a more complete picture to emerge it is necessary to see the earlier publications and to regard *East Grinstead and its Environs* as a sequel to them.

I have tried to show some of the social life of the town and its surroundings – people appear in most of the pictures. The chapter headings indicate something of this: the shops people used; the activities in which they were involved; the houses in which they lived; the people themselves – some of them prominent personalities, some totally unknown; some of the schools they attended and the games they played; and the transport they used – trains, buses, cars. Many of the photographs have been published for the first time.

Now to the title: this is a tribute to East Grinstead's first-ever guide book, *A History and Guide to East Grinstead and its Environs*, written and illustrated by William Reynolds Pepper and published in December 1885 by Farncombe & Co., the Lewes-based proprietors of the town's then leading newspaper, *the East Grinstead Observer*. Pepper was born at Brighton around 1830 and during the late 1860s and early 1870s ran the King's Head at Pound Hill; by the late 1870s he had moved to East Grinstead where, residing at No. 2 Moat Terrace (the present No. 191 London Road), he was an artist, portrait painter and journalist. It is believed that he compiled his *History and Guide* as a speculative venture and persuaded Farncombe's to publish it but, although it met with a certain amount of success, the cost of its publication was greater than the money made from sales, Pepper himself almost certainly making nothing out of it even if Farncombe's did. As a journalist he was probably freelance and contributed a two-part Christmas story to the *East Grinstead Observer* entitled *The Guest at the Crown – a tale of East Grinstead 70 years ago*. This appeared in the issues dated 25 December 1880 and 1 January 1886. By 1891 Pepper had moved to No. 14 North End, near Felbridge, by which time he was sixty, and he died probably only a few years afterwards.

Copies of Pepper's book are very rare and have been for a great many years; fortunately a battered copy survives in East Grinstead Town Museum complete with advertisments. The text gives a brief history of the town together with a description of the High Street and other major features. There is an itinerary of local walks – 'a series of routes for tourists in the neighbourhood' – and finally a guide to the new railway opened in 1884 from Oxted to East Grinstead, though the suggestion has been made that Pepper did not write this part and that it may have been reprinted from London, Brighton & South Coast Railway promotional literature. The book is enlivened by several of Pepper's pen and ink sketches, some of which are reproduced in these pages. The guide has great charm and is written in a 'chatty style', its descriptions interspersed with anecdotes and folk lore, some of which are very amusing. Here is one about a gentleman tourist visiting Brambletye ruins and conversing with a local yokel:

'Ah, my lad, I suppose an old castle formerly stood here?' 'No it warn't,' was the reply. 'What, then?' was the further enquiry. 'Why it was formerly a new one,' replied the rustic, with a broad grin.'

Pepper has a noteworthy comment on the nearby Brambletye crossing:

'Leaving the ancient memento of past grandeur of which we have been speaking, we turn to the right and a road takes us to a railway crossing and gatehouse. The person in charge at the time of our visit was the innocent cause of a dreadful accident which occurred in Clayton Tunnel some years since, while fulfilling the office of signalman. Poor old fellow, it was quite a misadventure; hence the company retained him for many years in their service.'

The Clayton Tunnel collision was on 25 August 1861 and the signalman responsible was Henry Killick.

Like many Victorians, Pepper was very keen that 'useless' plots of land, such as Ashdown Forest, should have houses built on them, and he was also most enthusiastic about the efficiency of East Grinstead's drainage system: 'The proof of the excellence of the drainage is in the death returns, which showed for the last year the surprisingly low rate of thirteen per thousand.' Such things were of great importance to Victorians.

However, be warned: Anyone lucky enough to obtain a copy of *History and Guide* might be disappointed to find, as town historian Patrick Wood did, that 'The historical content is not of great value… The author's style is repellent; the reader is constantly assailed with bad puns… arch and tiresome to read… The book has not much value as a work of reference.'

In the present work every photograph is credited, where known, to its photographer or, in the case of a picture post card, to its original publisher. Pictures credited 'TM' are the property of East Grinstead Town Museum, photographer unknown. Where no credit is shown it means that unfortunately I have been unable to ascertain the identity of the photographer; many such pictures turn up at the Town Museum and if the donors themselves have no idea of 'who, what or when' it is seldom indeed that anyone else is likely to know.

David Gould
May 2001

One
East Grinstead Overviews

The town centre as seen from the top of St Swithun's church tower, 1932. The west end of the High Street is seen running bottom left of the picture, with the imposing bulk of Constitutional Buildings near the centre. Beyond is the junction of West Street and Ship Street, with the Ship inn clearly visible. In the distance, nestling in the trees, is Hill Place railway viaduct. (Harold Connold)

East Grinstead looking north, *c.* 1921. Prominent is St Swithun's parish church and, to its left, the cattle market and Cantelupe Road, with the High Street running across the picture and the Crown Hotel clearly visible. Top right are the council schools, now rebuilt as Chequer Mead Arts Centre. (Surrey Flying Services series, Croydon)

Part of the town, looking north-east, *c.* 1935. The largest of the three gasholders is shown on the 1936, but not the 1931, edition of the OS map. St Michael's College may be seen immediately to the north-east of the gasholders; St Margaret's Junction is top left ; and Park Road is bottom left where can also be seen the three-gabled London Transport bus garage in Garland Road. (TM)

Railway station, *c.* 1921. Running from top left to bottom centre is the London to Lewes line, serving the low-level station; and running from bottom left to top right is the Three Bridges to Tunbridge Wells line, serving the high-level station. Also visible is the low-level goods yard, rail-connected to the high-level yard, which was opposite John Stenning & Son's timber yard. London Road runs from left to right near the top of the picture. (Surrey Flying Services series, Croydon)

London Road, looking north-west from St Swithun's church tower, *c*. 1964. The town clock, mounted on its tower built in 1955, stands at 3.43 and immediately behind this, the Three Bridges to Tunbridge Wells railway passes beneath the road. Beyond the A.1 Shoe Co.'s shop is the old White Lion, which was rebuilt in 1965. The quantity of motor vehicles around was about normal for the mid-1960s. (Chris Crosthwaite)

Two
Commerce

Jubilee Institute and public coffee bar, No. 57 London Road, 1937. This building was opened in November 1888, the librarian and manager of the coffee bar being William Harding until his death in 1922. William Bright then took over the same duties until 1938, when the building was demolished. The cafe was said to have served the best tea and sandwiches in town; the window labels read 'Cooked Ham' and 'Eggs and Bacon'. Incidentally the clock, originally mounted above the right-hand upper window, was soon moved to the position seen here where it could be observed more easily by people coming from the High Street end of town. (Harold Connold)

Number 30 Cantelupe Road which was from around 1904-1909 the home of Henry Walter Cullen, printer. Run by his executors after his death, Cullens produced high-quality printing in the shed, seen on the right, for almost all local businesses, including Sargents of East Grinstead, whose former bus garage is seen on the left. Cullens closed in 1960 and in January 1971 S. Taylor, jewellers, opened here. (D. Gould)

Cullen's

EAST GRINSTEAD
332

J. S. CULLEN   P. W. CULLEN

General & Commercial

PRINTERS &
STATIONERS

30 CANTELUPE ROAD
EAST GRINSTEAD

★   PRINTERS   OF   THIS   PROGRAMME   ★

Advertisement, printed by Cullens, from the East Grinstead Operatic Society's programme in November 1953. This firm printed all the society's programmes, which by including many such advertisements were able to be sold at low cost. (TM)

14

William Curtis's baker's boy, possibly a member of his own extensive family, c. 1910. Curtis, born in Brighton around 1851, came to East Grinstead and established his grocer's and baker's shop at No. 137 West Street around 1885. He opened another shop, at No. 86 London Road, in 1896, moving to No. 94 (the present No. 104) in 1907. He handed over the West Street shop to Henry Thwaites around 1908, Albert Curtis then ran it during the 1920s and 1930s.

Curtis's bakery, No. 16 De la Warr Road, 1920s. The adjoining grocery shop opened around 1908 and was on the corner of Chequer Road. Not only was bread made here but also very sticky-looking cakes and buns, which were sold at Curtis's 'refreshment rooms' at No. 104 London Road.

Cruttenden, Sawyers & Co.

Oldest Firm in the Town—Established 1777

PRACTICAL WATCH & CLOCK MAKERS

REPAIRS of every
description a speciality

Old Gold and Silver Bought

46 HIGH STREET, EAST GRINSTEAD

Telephone 493

Advertisement from *East Grinstead – the Official Guide*, 1948. Thomas Jenner Cruttenden & Co. first appeared at No. 29a London Road around 1906, taking over the business of Albert Winser, watchmaker. Then, as Cruttenden, Sawyers & Co., it moved to No. 25 London Road around 1920. This shop was bombed during the war, necessitating a move to No. 46 High Street where the business remained until the mid-1960s.

The Direct Meat Supply Co., *c.* 1928. This establishment, at No. 44 London Road, was somewhat short-lived, being in business from the mid 1920s to the mid 1930s. The formidable-looking proprietor invites customers to 'Try Our Famous Davies' Bacon' and 'Watch Our Windows For Lucky Numbers'. (TM)

Thomas Duke, confectioner, at the entrance to his shop at No. 28 London Road, *c.* 1902. He ran the business here, having moved from West Street where he was a tailor and currier, from the mid-1880s to the early 1920s. His neighbour Arthur Wood, a piano dealer, was in business from the mid-1880s to around 1902. (TM)

The shop of William John Heath, tailor and hatter, which was at No. 78 Glen Vue Road from around 1904-1909. Like his neighbour he is celebrating Empire Day (24 May) in great style. Heath's first shop was at No. 75 High Street from 1890-1903. Glen Vue Road was renamed Railway Approach in 1906, and the whole building was demolished around 1963.

East Grinstead Gas & Water Co.

*What is the **greatest aid** to the comfort, leisure and pleasure of the busy **Housewife?***

Answer:—*The full application of gas to the household needs.*

GAS for Cooking—Cheap, Clean, Convenient, Economical.

GAS for Heating—No Coal to carry, no ashes, no dust.

GAS for Hot Water—Always ready " on tap."

GAS Copper for Washing—Banishes wash-day worries.

GAS Iron—Gives wash-day a smooth and comfortable finish.

GAS for Bath—Ready any hour, day or night, 'round the clock.'

For these comforts apply :—

EAST GRINSTEAD GAS & WATER COMPANY,

SHOW ROOMS   ::   LONDON ROAD

Advertisement from Cullen's Directory, 1928. The East Grinstead Gas & Water Co. was a limited liability company formed by an Act of Parliament in 1878. There were separate managers for the gasworks and the water works (opened in 1880). Electric lighting, run by the Urban District Council, began to supersede gas lighting from 1923.

East Grinstead Gas & Water Co. showroom on London Road, *c.* 1920. It was situated between the railway bridge and the brewery (on whose site stands the present fire station). For many years the gas manager was D.T. Livesey and the water manager was R.G. Payne, but by 1930 one man, John Hyde, combined the posts of secretary, engineer and manager. (TM)

An apparently new Morris lorry of C. & H. Gasson Ltd, registered in 1960. This firm of builders' merchants owned two lorries, for mainly local deliveries, and both are seen in Gasson's yard at No. 153 London Road. On the right is George Ernest Leppard (1903-1978), one of Gasson's drivers from around 1930-1966. A native of East Grinstead, he was one of the 'earlier generations of *locals* who really were local – before all the outside influences came along.' (Courtesy of M.J. Leppard)

The Bakery at No. 91 Lingfield Road on its last day, 14 May 1988. A regular customer has just bought her final loaf of bread here. There had been a bakery here since the mid-1880s, the first proprietor being T. Groombridge, followed by William Ledword (around 1890-1930), Charles Simmons (1930s-1970s) and finally Peter and Jan Litchfield. (D. Gould)

Advertisement from William *Pepper's History and Guide to East Grinstead and its Environs*, 1885. George Henry Lynn was born in East Grinstead in March 1848, the son of George Lynn, builder, brickmaker and potter, at No. 46 High Street. Much of G.H. Lynn's work may be examined in the sadly neglected Queens Road Cemetery. A noted cricketer, at one time he appeared in the Sussex County XI. In September 1921 G.H. Lynn died in the house in which he had been born.

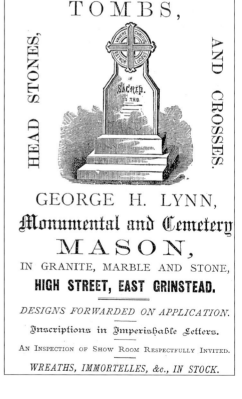

TOMBS,

HEAD STONES,

AND CROSSES.

GEORGE H. LYNN,

Monumental and Cemetery

MASON,

IN GRANITE, MARBLE AND STONE,

HIGH STREET, EAST GRINSTEAD.

DESIGNS FORWARDED ON APPLICATION.

Inscriptions in Imperishable Letters.

AN INSPECTION OF SHOW ROOM RESPECTFULLY INVITED.

WREATHS, IMMORTELLES, &c., IN STOCK.

East Grinstead Market, Cantelupe Road, c. 1960. Here, local farmers could buy and sell livestock, mainly cattle, sheep and pigs. William Rudge, an auctioneer, founded this market in around 1870 and the firm of Turner Rudge & Turner, estate agents and auctioneers, always owned it. (TM)

The market in Gantelupe Road, c. 1960. An employee is driving the sheep into their pens ready for sale. (TM)

At the Market, Cantelupe Road, *c.* 1960. These girls find two lambs irresistibly cuddly, but would they be eating lamb for lunch a short while later? (TM)

Raymond Wood (1900-1979), auctioneer at the Cattle Market from 1954 to 1967, in characteristic pose *c.* 1960. A native of East Grinstead, he was senior partner in Turner Rudge & Turner and became an authority on vernacular architecture; he wrote *A Short Account of Sackville College*. By 1970 the market was small and uneconomic to run, so on 10 December 1970 East Grinstead's final Fat Stock Show was held, Mr Wood coming out of retirement to sell the last bullock. (TM)

Saturday Market in Railway Approach, *c.* 1993. This weekly stall market, inaugurated by the town mayor, Philip Briggs, began on 18 February 1989 and was well used at first. There had not been such a market in the town since May 1982, when the one operating on the former cattle market site in Cantelupe Road closed down. (TM)

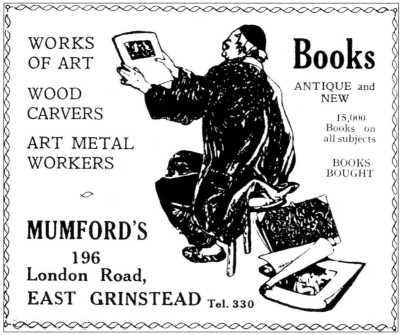

WORKS
OF ART

WOOD
CARVERS

ART METAL
WORKERS

MUMFORD'S
196
London Road,
EAST GRINSTEAD Tel. 330

Books

ANTIQUE and
NEW

15,000
Books on
all subjects

BOOKS
BOUGHT

Advertisement from town guide, *c.* 1931. David T. Mumford opened his first antique shop in 1922 in Railway Approach, also doing art metalwork and woodcarving. He moved to larger premises at No. 196 London Road in 1929, then from 1935 to the late 1950s was at No. 192 London Road, specialising in rare books. Among his customers were John Betjeman, Cyril Fletcher, Tony Hancock and Patrick Moore.

Rice Bros. shop at Nos 29/31 London Road, *c.* 1905. The brothers were Thomas, a harness maker, and Joseph, a saddler and agricultural implement maker; there was also Alfred Rice, a carriage builder. Rice Bros., new in 1891, also sold bicycles, and became a limited company in July 1893. To the right of the shop is the Warwick Arms, behind which on a higher level are some very early cottages. All were destroyed in 1943 and 1944. (Arthur Harding)

One of London Road's landmarks: this carved oak boot which hung over Russell & Bromley's shop until recently. Here T. Pither (left) and Michael Boyce – who had restored and regilded the boot – are about to rehang it on 4 October 1972. Previously it had hung over Martha Walker's shoe shop at No. 60 London Road. (*East Grinstead Observer*)

John Stenning & Son Ltd, timber merchants and sawmill proprietors, 1945. Harold Leppard, the engineer in charge, is minding a British Thomson-Houston electricity generator, which was driven by steam, fired by offcuts of timber; the steam also being used for the works' hooter. This family business, originally established in 1792, became a limited liability company in July 1900 and closed in 1964, though operations continued in Robertsbridge for a few more years. (TM)

Lilian Daisy Styles (1905-1992), fruiterer and greengrocer, 1975. Her shop was at No. 44 High Street from 1928 to 1981, when she gave up because the property owners required an increase in the rent. She also ran the Bays Nursery, Godstone Road, Lingfield from 1949 to 1986 (when she was eighty-one). In her youth she was a top athlete and six times national cross-country champion. (*East Grinstead Observer*)

Wood's hardware store at No. 186 London Road, *c.* 1905. It was here from around 1904 to 1927. On display are domestic crockery, saucepans, jugs, teapots, Zeimar gas mantles, buckets, brushes and shovels. William John Wood (1865-1938) was a member of St Swithun's Parochial Church Council and a sidesman. (TM)

EAST GRINSTEAD   *Dorset Arms Hotel*

The Dorset Arms Hotel, a pencil drawing by Leslie J. Tyler, c. 1927. This inn, mainly eighteenth century, was earlier called The Catt; earlier names for the inn on the site were the Newe Inn, then the *Ounce* (1605). In the 1930s, when the proprietor was W. Chattey, it was one of the few Sussex inns in private ownership. The name Dorset Arms dates from the 1780s.

The Swan Inn, London Road, *c.* 1902. Although one of East Grinstead's most attractive public houses, it was closed in February 1963 and pulled down shortly afterwards, being replaced in November 1964 by three shops, one of which was a gas showroom. W. Venn's butcher's shop was very short-lived and by 1903 W. & H. King, cyclemakers, had moved in. (TM)

Whitehall theatre, picture house and restaurant, London Road, 1914. In 1910 Letheby &
Christopher, the Ascot caterers, acquired the Grosvenor Hall (built in 1883 and first used on
11 February 1884) and converted the premises into a cinema, East Grinstead's first. The picture
palace began operations on 8 November 1910, with seats at 1s 9d and 6d, and there was a Grand
Opening Concert the next day. In 1936 the Whitehall was further rebuilt with the extended
frontage that still stands, necessitating the destruction of three cottages known as Rock
Gardens. (F. Frith & Co.)

WHITEHALL PALACE

EAST GRINSTEAD.

UND .R THE DIRECT MANAGEMENT OF THE PROPRIETORS.

WHERE EVERYBODY GOES.

The BRIGHTEST SPOT in EAST GRINSTEAD

Comfort—Courtesy—Consistency.

BOX OFFICE—TEL. NO. 82, E.G.

GENERAL MANAGER — — — FRED. C. MAPLESDEN

The opulent interior of the Whitehall theatre and cinema, from the guidebook *East Grinstead*, 1926. There were six chandeliers, and the decor included classical murals. Above the stage may be discerned the seal of arms of East Grinstead. All was destroyed in the bombing of 9 July 1943, when 108 people died. (TM)

D. & P. Humphrey, family butcher, North Street, Turners Hill, July 1983. This engaging little building is at the north end of the village, which stands at a crossroads 558 ft above sea level. (D. Gould)

An attractive but definitely dated advertisement by a Lingfield sweet-shop proprietor, 1960. Even then, Lingfield schoolchildren did not use the term 'tuck' for sweets!

Three
Events and Occasions

Fundraising fête for East Grinstead's new Queen Victoria Hospital, 7 August 1933. Sir Robert Kindersley declares the fête open; it made a profit of £607 and there were donations amounting to £1,600. From left to right : Lady Kindersley, Sir Robert, Admiral Sir Charles Madden, Captain J.P. Price, W. Guthrie Kirkhope, E. Leslie Steer. The hospital was opened on 8 January 1936. Robert Molesworth Kindersley (1871-1954) was chairman of Lazard Bros. & Co., the international bankers, and from 1920 to 1946 presided over the National Savings Committee. He received a KBE in 1917 and was created Baron in 1941. (Harold Connold)

East Grinstead fire brigade and horse-drawn Shand Mason engine at Imberhorne Park, 1905. Each year the brigade competed for the challenge cup, which it won in 1905 and 1913. These fire brigade shows were major events and well attended by the public. (Arthur Harding)

Memorial procession in De la Warr Road, *c.* 1910. The East Grinstead Military and Town Band, followed by the Territorials, is marching from the Armoury – now called Huntingdon Hall – at the east end of the road. In the background is W. Curtis's grocery shop and his adjoining bakery, on the corner of Chequer Road. (Arthur Harding)

Destruction of the Whitehall Cinema, London Road, 9 July 1943. A lone raider dropped a stick of bombs across the town and 108 people, most of whom were in the cinema, were killed. Here we see the remains of the cinema interior and proscenium. (*East Grinstead Observer*)

Further wartime destruction, this time caused by a flying bomb that had been shot down, falling on London Road, 12 July 1944. The explosion destroyed the remaining structures on the east side of the road, while the blast severely damaged shops on the west side. These were No. 32 Timothy Whites & Taylors; chemists; No. 34 Dewhurst, butcher; No. 34a Bobbie's Cafe and No. 36 the former North Sussex Garage, which the fire brigade was using during the war. Also visible are Canadian Army lorries, marked with a star. (*Kent & Sussex Courier*)

VE Day street party in Queens Road, 8 May 1945. This event was prepared in a great hurry overnight for around fifty children who were living on or near the road. Allen Tugwell, in top hat and tails seen bending over the table, provided entertainment. (TM)

Carnival float at Halsford Croft, 1949. The 'superstructure' has been built around a small lorry, whose cab makes quite an effective 'bridge'. The vehicle is believed to have been the entry of local coal merchants William Best & Son.

Members and supporters of the Liberal Party outside their local office at No. 92 Railway Approach, October 1949. Fourth from the right is John C. McLaughlin, wine importer and the party's parliamentary candidate. The lady with the posy is believed to be Mrs Byers of Hunters Hill, Blindley Heath, wife of Frank Byers MP. Extreme left is Elizabeth Cullen, widow of H.W. Cullen the local printer. (TM)

Scene from the pageant of East Grinstead, 1951. This was enacted in the grounds of East Court from 2-7 July as part of the Festival of Britain. The 'priest' in the centre is Peter Griffits, who died in 1997. (*Sussex Express & County Herald*)

A 'brass-hat' visiting the Lewes Road headquarters of East Grinstead Air Training Corps 1343 Squadron, c. 1950. This squadron was formed in February 1941. Here, Air Marshall Sir Ronald Ivelaw-Chapman talks to Flt-Sgt Peter Lindfield. Sir Ronald (1899-1978) had a long and distinguished career in the Royal Air Force, being awarded a DFC in 1918, a CBE in 1943 and KBE in 1951, when he was commander-in-chief of the Indian Air Force. He retired in 1957. (TM)

St Luke's Sunday School outing to Littlehampton just before departure at Stone Quarry, *c.* 1959. The party, which is about to board a hired Southdown coach, includes parents and helpers and church secretary Sidney Holloway Standing, (a cousin of the actor Stanley Holloway) is seeing them off. The left-hand group of four girls in the foreground includes the two Tyler sisters; the right-hand group of three girls includes Sally Dighton. The five ladies on the extreme right are Mrs Gibbs, Mrs Dighton, Mrs Young, Mrs Yates and possibly Mrs Daley. (*East Grinstead Courier*)

Chamber of Commerce Exhibition at the Whitehall, London Road, c. 1960. At the microphone is Richard 'Stinker' Murdoch, the popular comedian of his day. From left to right, front row: -?-, -?-, Clemence Hartigan, Cllr John Stenning (chairman of the Urban District Council 1959-1960), Mrs B. Preece, Murdoch, B. Preece, Mr Wilson. (*East Grinstead Observer*)

Filming a scene for the TV serial *Colditz* at Ashdown Park, November 1973. Apparently the fabric of this former Notre Dame Convent, by 1973 the United States International University, was considered suitable to stand in for Colditz Castle. (*East Grinstead Observer*)

Demolition of shops on the corner of London Road and West Street, 1964. 'Cosy Corner', one of the oldest confectionery shops in East Grinstead – owned by Maurice Pullinger – has already gone, having closed on 1 February 1964, and P.J. May the estate agents are next to disappear, albeit temporarily. By August 1965 P.J. May were back in new premises on the same site. The town suffered very badly in the mid-1960s, as did many other places, from unnecessary redevelopment. (Chris Crosthwaite)

A heartbreaking sight: demolition of Nos 30/32 High Street during February 1968. This fifteenth-century timber-framed shop, formerly the premises of H.S. Martin & Co., chemists, was a listed building of historical interest, yet East Grinstead Urban District Council's Planning Committee approved its demolition, the result of which spoiled what had been an unbroken line of medieval structures. To guard against any further depredations the East Grinstead Society was founded in April 1968. (Chris Crosthwaite)

Opening of the East Grinstead Society's exhibition 'A Look at East Grinstead', Chequer Mead school, 21 July 1975. From left to right: Geoffrey Johnson Smith, MP for East Grinstead 1965-1983 and president of the society; Dennis Jefferies, exhibition organizer and committee member; and Michael Leppard MA, chairman of the society 1974-1978. They are viewing a model of Estcots housing estate. (*East Grinstead Observer*)

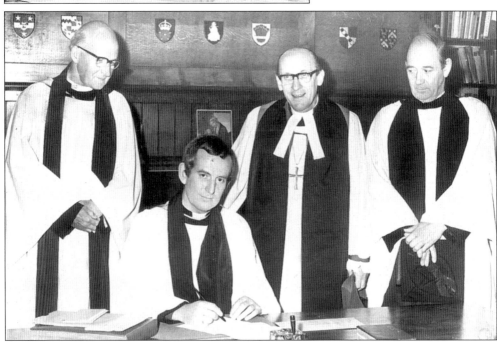

Induction of the Revd John Roger Brown as vicar of East Grinstead, October 1975. He replaced Canon Harry Copsey who had been vicar since 1954. From left to right: the Revd Peter Curgenwen, rural dean of East Grinstead; Revd Roger Brown; the Right Revd I. Colin Docker, bishop of Horsham; the Venerable F.G. Kerr-Dineen, archdeacon of Horsham. Mr Brown was vicar until July 1997. (*East Grinstead Observer*)

East Grinstead Young Conservatives' float, part of the annual Carnival procession, 31 August 1981. The lorry, carrying a fanciful miniature castle, is passing the Roman Catholic church in London Road and will end its journey at East Court. These events ceased after 1984. (D. Gould)

Carnival procession in College Lane, 27 August 1984. Led by the town mayor, Cllr Alan Collinge, and the President of the Lions, Ernie Huggett, it left the railway station at 1.30 p.m., went up Railway Approach and London Road, and along the High Street and College Lane to the grounds of East Court. Behind the Carnival Queen is the band of the Nautical Training Corps. (D. Gould)

Opening of the exhibition 'Our Town 1884-1984' at the Scout Hall, Moat Road, 30 July 1984. From left to right: Roger Horman; Cllr Veronica Horman, deputy mayor of East Grinstead; Dr Raymond Crawfurd, of Tenterden, who officially opened the exhibition; and Michael Leppard, pointing at a large model of the town in 1884 made by Ronald Michell, chief organizer of the exhibition. *(East Grinstead Courier)*

Four
Royal Visits

Queen Elizabeth, the Queen's Mother, opening the new children's ward at the Queen Victoria Hospital, East Grinstead, 6 July 1955. Named the Pea-Nut Ward, and built by the local firm of W.H. Price (Builders) Ltd, it was at the west-end of the Dewar Ward. In addition to the lines of nurses some members of the Red Cross may be seen. (TM)

FLYING BOMB HITS TOWN

Visit of the King and Queen

FEW CASUALTIES

Early on Wednesday a flying bomb crashed on the site where a bomb fell over a year ago in a town in Southern England. The casualties were light. Three people were killed and a few were injured by flying glass.

The incident occurred in a road, the blast destroying shop premises on each side of the street. The road was littered with glass. Nobody was in the shops at the time and the three people killed were in the road. They ran for cover, but were too late.

Several others had narrow escapes, and owe their lives to the fact that they fell flat in the roadway.

Shop windows in the street were blown out, and many houses were similarly damaged.

An eye-witness said: "I saw what was going to happen. The engine of the bomb cut out. I jumped off my cycle and lay flat down. Next I heard the crash, which was deafening, followed by the falling glass. Never shall I forget the noise."

Within a few moments following the incident, the Civil Defence workers and members of the Women's Voluntary Services and Home Guard were at work on the scene, and proprietors, managers and staffs of businesses had their coats off, clearing the debris. All worked splendidly, and they greatly appreciated the tea supplied from the Women's Voluntary Services' mobile canteen. Another much appreciated service was that of the Traders' Mutual Assistance organisation.

VISIT OF KING AND QUEEN

In the midst of the clearing work came—as a complete surprise — the King and Queen, who immediately stopped the Royal car and together walked up and down the main road. They were given a great ovation.

Their Majesties met many A.R.P. workers and chatted with them, including the Chief Air Raid Warden, whom the King recognised as an ex-London police officer. They spoke also to the Women's Voluntary Services organiser, Miss Wallis and several others.

"It did me good," said one of the victims of the incident, who had lost his business. "They were both charming, and one felt the deep sincerity of their sympathy."

The King at once asked to see the actual spot where the bomb fell, and when told of the coincidence was struck by the calm way in which everybody was taking things.

"I think you are all splendid," his Majesty remarked.

The Queen in her turn talked to many women, and was specially interested in the salvage work that was going on.

As one of the crowd was heard to say nothing could have helped the town so much at that moment as the inspiring presence of—to quote his words—"Our beloved King and Queen."

Complete report of the visit of King George VI and Queen Elizabeth to East Grinstead shortly after the flying bomb had fallen on London Road on 12 July 1944. It is from the *East Grinstead Observer* dated Saturday 15 July 1944. The paper did its best to disguise the town's identity but local readers would have known all too well. The chief air raid warden referred to was T. Peters.

Princess Margaret attending the Royal Gala Performance of Ballet at the Adeline Genée Theatre, 29 January 1967. It was the opening night of this ultra-modern theatre, just outside the town at Baldwins Hill, Surrey. The princess, accompanied by her then husband Lord Snowdon, is talking to Stanley Holden. (*East Grinstead Courier*)

Princess Margaret talking to Dame Margot Fonteyn at the Adeline Genée Theatre, 29 January 1967. This great ballerina, whose real name was Margaret Hookham, was born at Reigate in 1919 and spent her entire career with the Royal Ballet. She was created a Dame in 1956 and died in 1991. The theatre, and its associated Bush-Davies dancing school, had a short life, being closed in July 1989. (*East Grinstead Courier*)

Prince Philip on a visit to the London Federation of Boys' Clubs, Hindleap Warren, Ashdown Forest, June 1975. He is talking to instructor John Morris, with Philip Levy at his side. Demonstrating his prowess on a rope – and upstaging the Duke of Edinburgh – is one of the boys from London. (*East Grinstead Observer*)

Prince Philip at Hindleap Warren, June 1975. He is accepting , on behalf of the Boys' Clubs, a 17-seat coach presented by the Variety Club of Great Britain Golfing Society. Leslie Macdonnell, chairman of the Sunshine Coach Scheme, does the honours. (*East Grinstead Observer*)

Five

Houses

East Grinstead looking west, August 1855. Sackville College (the almshouse founded in 1609), together with its chapel, is on the skyline and on the left is the tower of St Swithun's parish church. In the foreground are the 'Cottages on the Rocks', long since demolished, in Old Road, which was the original eastern approach to the town. This scene is one of a series of the earliest known photographs of East Grinstead. (TM)

Sackville College from the quadrangle, looking north, August 1855. The family of the warden, the Revd John Mason Neale, poses for the photographer Joseph Cundall (1818-1895). Seated by the wall, from left to right: Sarah Agnes, Mrs Neale, Margaret Isobel, Cornelius Vincent, J.M Neale. Crouching on the ground are Katherine Ermenild and Mary Sackville Neale. (TM)

Sackville College main entrance, August 1855. In the doorway stands 'Master' William Wren, the porter, in his long apron. The seated figure is wearing a 'round frock' commonly known as smock. Ivy, once considered a picturesque adornment, is no longer tolerated because of the damage it causes to the fabric.

Old houses in East Grinstead High Street, east end, as seen by William Reynolds Pepper (from *History and Guide*, 1885). Prominent on the left is Cromwell House; the houses right of centre that were later demolished to make way for the entry of Portland Road; the shop with quill pen-shaped windows at the end of Middle Row; and right, the Rose beerhouse.

Two drawings of Sackville College by W.R Pepper, from his *History and Guide*, 1885. *Left*: the quadrangle showing Dorset Lodgings, with exaggerated perspective, looking north. *Right*: the south front, viewed from the High Street.

Sackville House, Nos 70-72 High Street, June 1939. Mainly fifteenth century, the house was later extended; its timber framing originally covered by plasterwork was exposed in 1919. The roof was raised in the seventeenth century but a tie beam marking the original roofline is still visible in one of the bedrooms. (Harold Connold)

A not entirely accurate drawing of Cromwell House (centre) and adjoining buildings in the High Street by R. H. Nibbs, *c.* 1860. Sackville and Amherst Houses (right) are shown somewhat compressed and with their windows in the wrong places, although one could argue that the artist – who has put his name on the fascia of Porch House (left) – was essaying a romanticised and over-picturesque view of the town. These house names were not in general use until the mid-1880s. (From *Antiquities of Sussex*, first series, 1874)

Stone privy, dating from the seventeenth century, at Porch House, Nos 82-84 High Street, c. 1968. Also at the rear of the house and not visible from the street is a seventeenth-century carved stone porch. The west-end of the house itself is early sixteenth century, the east-end frontage being late sixteenth century. (P.D. Wood)

The Round Houses, at the west-end of the High Street, looking west, 1890. A group of four back-to-back dwellings, also known as West Buildings, they were demolished in spring 1891; Constitutional Buildings (built 1893) now stand on their site. (William Page)

Cottages, Nos 159-161 London Road, c. 1963. They are believed to have been built in the late sixteenth or early seventeenth century and later extended. Known as Thunder Hall until the late nineteenth century they stood immediately south-east of the White Lion inn (left). They came down in June 1967. (M.J. Leppard)

Southwick House, London Road, April 1983. This villa was built around 1887, its first occupant being Henry Heasman, a farmer, who lived here until the early 1920s. In 1950 East Sussex County Council, having bought the house for £800, converted the lower floor into a public branch library (the upper floor was let as flats) which opened on 21 June 1950 and was closed on 13 December 1983. (D. Gould)

Cottages known as Rock Gardens, Nos 49, 51 and 53 London Road, 1934. William Wood, one of East Grinstead's postmen, lived in the centre house from around 1850 to 1881. For many years it was the practice to announce the results of General Elections from the front gardens to crowds who had assembled in London Road. In 1934-1935 the cottages were demolished and the Whitehall (right) was given a new extended frontage, with a parade of shops, restaurant and cinema being opened in April 1936. On the left can be seen part of the Jubilee Institute, which lasted until 1938. The large posters on the wall fronting Rock Gardens advertise films being shown at the Whitehall – *Ever Since Eve* with George O'Brien, *David Harum* with Will Rogers, *Mandalay*, with Kay Francis and *George White's Scandals* with Rudy Vallee — all of which were made in 1934. (Harold Connold)

Derelict farmhouse at what is now the junction of Park and Grosvenor Roads, *c.* 1905. In the 1890s this was Copyhold Farm but earlier it was known as Killick's Farm. William Best the coal merchant bought the whole property and sold it for house-building, and 'Hucknall' was named after the Nottinghamshire pit from which Best purchased his coal.

Millfield, Windmill Lane, April 1989. This was built a few yards south-west of the site of a windmill in around 1912. From 1946-1961 a newspaper strip-cartoon scriptwriter, John Henry Gordon Freeman, lived here. As 'Gordon Grinstead' he also wrote for the famous boys' weekly *Eagle* from 1960 to 1962 (see p. 71). (D. Gould)

Imberhorne, north-east elevation, *c*. 1904. In 1872 Thomas F. Campbell purchased the estate of Imberhorne, nearly 531 acres, for £16,500. He then built this large house and sold it to Edward C. Blount, a banker and railway promoter. Knighted in 1878, Sir Edward died at Imberhorne in 1905 aged ninety-six. (William Page)

Imberhorne, south elevation, possibly early 1950s. Sir Edward Blount's grandson Edward had the house enlarged after 1905 and it remained in family ownership until his death in 1953. To pay the death duties his two daughters had to sell the house and grounds, and demolition came around 1956, followed by construction of a large housing estate. (Aero Enterprises, Westminster)

Ruins of Brambletye House, from a water-colour painting by James Lambert II, 1782. Sir Henry Compton began construction of the house – it has a date panel 1631 – but it may never have been completed. By 1700 decay had started though the front was still mostly complete in 1780. The gateway on the left had disappeared by the 1860s.

A drawing of Brambletye House dated 1830. By then one of the towers had been pulled down with an ox team to obtain material for road building nearby – presumably the 'Brambletye Bends' of 1826. The ruins became a tourist attraction after publication of Horace Smith's novel *Brambletye House* in 1826. The house looks much the same now.

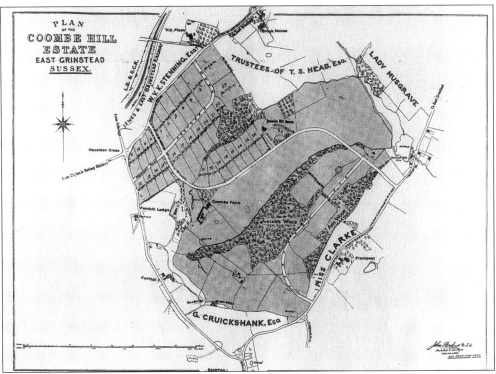

Plan of proposed Coombe Hill Estate, from a brochure, c. 1910. It shows thirty-one plots and the private Coombe Hill Road winding its way from Turners Hill Road to West Hoathly Road, plus the names of owners of adjacent property. Of the side roads shown, only Medway Drive was actually laid out. (Plan by John Rowland MSA, architect and surveyor, Old Charlton, Kent)

Cover of the brochure, describing in glowing terms the proposed Coombe Hill Estate. Although houses were indeed built along Coombe Hill Road those planned for the northern part of the estate never appeared. (TM)

Plan and artist's impression of one of the less-expensive freehold residences intended for Coombe Hill Estate. This one was offered for £1,500, its floor plan measuring 40 ft by 36 ft. The plan shows six bedrooms, a drawing room, morning room, dining room and kitchen. (TM)

Another freehold residence planned for Coombe Hill Estate, c. 1910. This one would have cost the buyer £2,000. The plan, which shows the house to be about 65 ft by 35 ft, includes five bedrooms, a hall, dining room, conservatory, drawing room and kitchen. The illustration depicts the almost inevitable Mock-Tudor style favoured, complete with battlements over the front door. (TM)

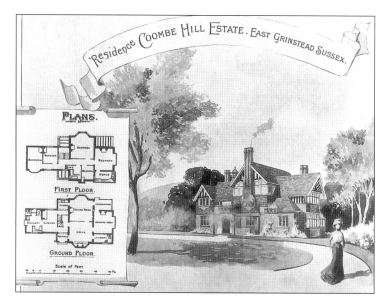

Ho Chee Almshouses, Dormansland, September 1975. Frank and Winnie Wallis are outside. John Ho Chee was the Chinese secretary to John Elphinstone, who was an East Indian merchant in the 1830s. Ho Chee died in March 1869 and his widow had the almshouses built in the early 1870s. (*East Grinstead Observer*)

Almshouses on the edge of Holtye golf course, September 1975. From left to right: Col. Reginald Grimes Metcalfe, Winifred Pannell and her husband James Pannell. (*East Grinstead Observer*)

Ashdown Park from the air, looking north-east, August 1974. Built for Thomas Thompson, the structure dates mainly from the 1870s and for some years was a private house. It has suffered many changes of ownership and use. From 1919 to 1969 it was the Notre Dame Convent; from 1971 to late 1973 it was in use as the United States International University; in 1974 Barclays Bank purchased the property and ran it as the Barclays Group Management Training Centre from 1976 to 1992; and since 1993 it has been the Ashdown Park Hotel. (TM)

Fen Place, near Turners Hill, c. 1955. The house was built in the latter part of the nineteenth century and soon extended. After the Second World War it became a retirement home, first for civil servants and later for Congregational ministers. It is now Alexander House Hotel. (Harold Connold)

Priest House
West Hoathly

(Sussex Archaeological Trust)

Interior of the Priest House, West Hoathly, April 1936. Since 1930 the house has been owned by the Sussex Archaeological Society and run as a museum. It is a fifteenth century timber-framed structure and had been a farmhouse since the sixteenth century. (Harold Connold)

Rowfant House, September 1974. The name means 'rough, bracken-covered land'. The house was built for Robert Whitfield, an ironmaster, in the late sixteenth century ; the central, three-gabled, E-shaped section is the original part. From 1848 Curtis Miranda Lampson (1806-1885) lived here; he had the house enlarged to the east and west some time after 1855, and included red brick imitation Tudor gables on the west side. When the Three Bridges to East Grinstead railway was being planned he sold the company land rather cheaply on condition a station was built to serve his house; the station was duly opened in July 1855. Lampson's son-in-law Frederick Locker-Lampson (1821-1895) also lived at Rowfant from 1874-1895; a great picture and book collector, he aimed to acquire first editions of English literature. In 1953 Oliver Locker-Lampson leased the house to the London Latvian Evangelical Lutheran Church and there were still twenty-three elderly Latvians living there in 1988. *(East Grinstead Observer)*

Mill Place Farm, Kingscote, May 1987. Its oldest part is late fourteenth century. The tenant farmer at this time was Alex Leggatt, an East Grinstead Town Councillor (mayor 1986-1987). His father Tom, who had farmed here before him, was an Urban District councillor (chairman 1958-1959). (D. Gould)

Saint Hill Farmhouse, Saint Hill Green, July 1983. This sandstone house was built in the 1860s by William Thomas Berger, who lived at Saint Hill from 1839 to 1872. Incidentally, the words 'Saint Hill' are pronounced with equal stress, and the name should not be rendered as 'St Hill Green' as certain direction signs do. (D. Gould)

Six
People

Ronald Michell (1916-1991) and his model of East Grinstead as it was in 1884, photographed in July 1984. Formerly assistant headmaster of Queen Mary's Hospital School, Carshalton, he came to live in East Grinstead in the late 1970s, becoming an active member of the East Grinstead Society. He frequently exhibited his models to the public and gave talks on local history; in 1983 he was a founder member of the Museum Society and its chairman from 1983 to 1991. (*East Grinstead Courier*)

Alexander John Baisden and his model of Imberhorne (or Hill Place) viaduct, February 1984. The East Grinstead Model Railway Club at this time was working on a large model of the railway station and its approaches, located in the basement at East Court, and this viaduct was his chief contribution. He died in January 1988 aged eighty-four. (*East Grinstead Courier*)

Albert Edward Best (1902-1985) at Halsford End, 14 October 1984. The youngest son of William Best – the East Grinstead coal and corn merchant whose business was established in 1887 – he and his sister Isabel took over the coal business in 1947, running it until October 1975. (D. Gould)

Ernest 'Joe' Dakin, 1930s. A native of Barnsley, he was manager of the East Grinstead branch of Louis G. Ford, builders merchants, from its opening in Brooklands Way on 5 August 1936 until his retirement in 1966. During the Second World War he was a special constable, and for ten years was a member of East Grinstead UDC and chairman 1955-1956; he was also a Rotarian. This well respected man died in 1983 aged seventy-nine. (A.E. Butler, Hailsham)

Mabel Louisa Evershed Dempster, 1946. She was a daughter of Dr Percy Evershed Wallis, who lived in Old Stone House from the late 1880s until 1921. In 1946 she was elected to the UDC and was its chairman during 1956-1957. By 1961 she was chairman of East Grinstead Girl Guides Association and served on the committee of East Grinstead Art Club. A founder member of the East Grinstead Society in 1968, this energetic lady died in 1975. (Harold Connold)

John Diffey (seated) and his splendid model of St Swithun's church, May 1960. The twelve-year-old, who had drawn his own plans from on-site measurements, displayed the model at a hobbies exhibition at the Parish Halls to raise money for the church. The boy on the right is setting an example by placing a coin in the slot. (*East Grinstead Observer*)

Leslie Dungey, one of East Grinstead's most prominent townsmen, *c*. 1950. He was a partner in Pearless, de Rougement & Co., solicitors. From 1941 he was with the Air Training Corps (1343 Squadron) first as adjutant then from 1945-1947 as C.O. with the rank of Flight Lieutenant. In 1944 he became a member of the UDC and was its chairman during 1948-1949; he was also a leading light in the Operatic Society. He died in March 1994. (Harold Connold)

John Henry Gordon Freeman (1903-1972), 1961. A staff writer on the *Daily Mirror*, 'Don' Freeman wrote the scripts for the daily strip cartoons 'Garth', 'Jane', 'Belinda' and 'Buck Ryan', as well as the children's page. As 'Gordon Grinstead' he wrote the serial 'Knights of the Road' for *Eagle* magazine from 1960 to 1962. A cultured and very private man, he was a member of the Sussex Archaeological Society. (*Daily Mirror*)

Sir Archibald Hector McIndoe, FRCS, opening the newly built Guinea Pig public house, 1957. New Zealand born, he arrived at East Grinstead's Queen Victoria Hospital in 1939 and was soon conducting plastic surgery on badly burned airmen – his Guinea Pigs, members of the world's most exclusive club, of which he became president. Knighted in June 1947, he died suddenly in April 1960 aged only fifty-nine. (*East Grinstead Observer*)

A simple but poignant message, December 1926. Writing to Mrs Leslie Wood (who was the enrolling member of the local Mothers' Union) A. Humphrey, of No. 131 Queens Road, informs her of Mrs Newnham's death on Tuesday 21 December. Unfortunately nothing is known of either the writer or the deceased. (TM)

> 131 Queens Road
> Tuesday.
> Dear Mrs Wood.
>   I am sorry
> to have to tell you we
> have lost another of our
> members by death
> Mrs Newnham was
> found dead this morning
> It is so sad for the
> family. yours very sincerely
>   A Humphrey

Mrs N.F. Nutt in the stableyard of Nutt Bros, riding and job masters, 16 March 1921. She was the wife of Harold Hewitt Nutt, whose brother Norman was a partner from 1905-1912. Harold's son Kenneth joined the business in 1922, by which time the landaus, broughams and victorias for hire had been joined by hire cars. The yard was at the bottom of Station Road, its site now a petrol station. (Ken Nutt)

SPENCER PERCIVAL.

PRIME MINISTER OF ENGLAND.

Married in the ruins of East Grinstead Church.
August 10th, 1790.

H. DANIELS,
STATIONER, ASSASSINATED IN THE HOUSE OF COMMONS, 1812.
EAST GRINSTEAD,

Spencer Perceval MA (1762-1812), from the painting by Sir W. Beechey, 1818. Born in London, Perceval visited East Grinstead once only, when he was married to Jane Wilson on 10 August 1790. He became MP for Northampton in 1796, supported Pitt, and was Prime Minister from 1809 until he was assassinated on 11 May 1812 at the House of Commons by John Bellingham, 'a man of disordered brain'. (TM)

Evelyn Prodger, aged thirteen. She was one of many children attending a matinée at the Whitehall Cinema on 9 July 1943 when a German bomb demolished the auditorium killing 108 people, of whom she was one. Her father was the manager of the East Grinstead branch of Freeman, Hardy & Willis Ltd at No. 2 Whitehall Parade, London Road. (TM)

Granny Smith, the hermit of Ashdown Forest, 1908. She lived in a canvas hut on the forest between Forest Row and West Hoathly for sixteen years and was seventy-eight when this photograph was taken. She had two cats for company and went round the country selling cotton and buttons. She paid a small rent to the farmers on whose land the hut stood. (W.H. Charlwood)

Nick Stephanakis outside Henry Goulden's bookshop, No. 24 High Street, 2 May 1983. Always known as 'Steph', he was East Grinstead's Youth Club leader from November 1950 until August 1985, hailing from Cardiff. A keen photographer until retirement, he made copies of many old local photographs and some of these are on display here. (D. Gould)

Herman Volk, aged ninety-one, January 1972. A son of the celebrated Magnus Volk of Brighton – builder of Britain's first electric railway – Herman lived at Link Cottage, Ship Street, East Grinstead. An aeronautical engineer who had flown aircraft since 1912, he never qualified as a pilot. Here he holds a model of a Tiger Moth – one of the aeroplanes he used to fly. (*East Grinstead Observer*)

Geoffrey Fuller Webb (1879-1954), renowned stained-glass window artist. He lived in Sackville House, Nos 70-72 High Street, from around 1920 to 1954. A devout Roman Catholic, he worked in both Anglican and Roman Catholic churches, his signature being in the form of a spider's web. Windows by him may be seen in St Mary's church, East Grinstead, and St John's church, Felbridge. Some of his posters are in the town museum's care. (TM)

Patrick Wood, founder member of the East Grinstead Society and its first chairman, January 1975. A chartered surveyor, he was a partner in East Grinstead estate agents Turner Rudge & Turner – the third generation of the Wood family. He did a great deal of work in unearthing the early history of the town, contributing many valuable (and readable) articles to the society's *Bulletin*. He moved to Scotland in 1994. (*East Grinstead Observer*)

Air Training Corps 1343 Squadron at the County (Grammar) School, 1946. From left to right, back row: -?-, -?-, -?-, Eddie Pitt, the PE instructor, Vic Allison, -?-, Pete Furminger, -?-. Back row: Geoff Roberts, Jack White LDS, Fred Cotcher, Bob Pucknell, -?-, -?-, Mick Hall, D. Morgan, -?-, -?-, Frank Steadman (engineering instructor), Bill Bax. Middle row: Tony Miles, Bob Roberts, ? Grey, Peter Pelling, Basil Gatton, Bentley Neale, Alan Huggett, John Crowhurst. Front row: Les Wilkinson, Peter Dyer, Vic Candish, Warrant Officer Frank Blanchard, Pilot Officer Brian Desmond (adjutant), Flt-Lt Leslie Dungey (C.O.), Flying Officer Patrick Moore, the drum-major, John Cook, Jack Smith. Apart from wartime service in the RAF (1940-1945) Patrick Moore lived in East Grinstead from 1927-1965 and for a time was a history master at a Tunbridge Wells preparatory school. He has presented *The Sky at Night* on BBC TV every month since 1957. (TM)

East Grinstead Fire Brigade, 1928. Seated at the wheel is B.G. Wheeler. From left to right, back row: George Simmons, J. Pentecost, F.R. Walker, A. Markwick, J.E. Power, W.J. Truckle, C. Pattenden, J.W. Brooker, J.C. Blackstone, W.H. Gobell, T.R. Blackstone. Front row: S.T. Brackpool, O.E. Perrin, G.S. Cooper, W. Truckle, William Simmons (captain), Tom Simmons, E.F. Simmons, G.F. Hills, A. Tomsett. George Simmons, who was the town's oldest fireman, died in August 1935 aged seventy-seven, having served on the brigade for fifty-two years; Arthur Tomsett died in January 1990 aged ninety-two. (TM)

Three clergymen, having packed their cases, sadly leave St Swithun's church, September 1960. Well, not really; this is a posed shot to illustrate what might happen if the clergy were sacked! From left to right: the Revd Graham Fuller (curate), the Revd Harry Copsey (vicar of East Grinstead 1954-1975), and the Revd Anthony Simpson (curate). (*Clarion Parish Magazine*)

A boy, possibly the photographer's son, cutting the sail on his model yacht at East Court boating pond, *c.* 1955. Frank S. Ashdown, a Sackville schoolmaster, was plainly a talented photographer but is reported also to have wielded the cane over-enthusiastically. Possibly because of his initials F.S. his charges referred to him as 'Fishy'. (F.S. Ashdown)

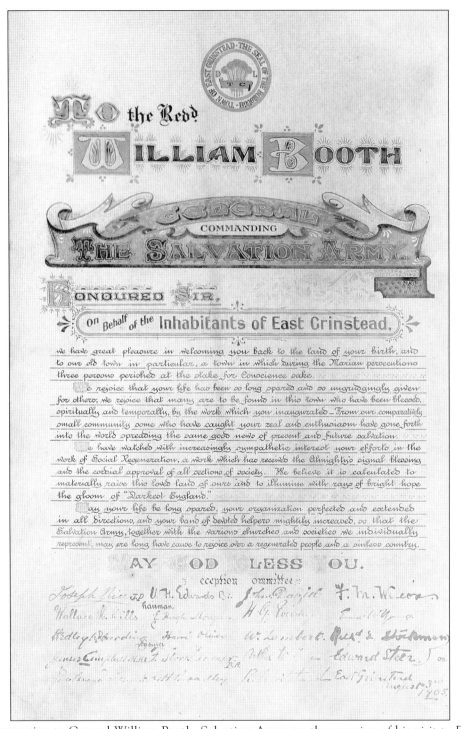

Presentation to General William Booth, Salvation Army, on the occasion of his visit to East Grinstead, 3 August 1905. It was signed by nineteen prominent townspeople, including Joseph Rice, chairman of the UDC; F.M. Wilcox, saddler; Wallace Hills, journalist; H.W. Harding, bank manager; and Edward Steer, builder. (Arthur Harding)

A cartoon relating to the General Election in East Grinstead, 25 January 1906. Some of the references are meaningless now, but it seems that the local football club had to cancel its match of 20 January because of the election, in which the Liberal candidate, C.H. Corbett, was to defeat the Conservative, E.M. Crookshank, by 262 votes. The label 'Women and Children Not Admitted' is a satirical allusion to the fact that such people could not vote. The 1906 Liberal victory – the only one in the town's history – was not unexpected, for the sender of the card on 23 January had written 'the eyes of the world will be upon this place next Thursday.' (drawing by A.B. True)

Moat Church members at the town's new police station at East Court, opened 23 June 1965. Some of the visitors look a trifle apprehensive! From left to right: police official, PC Keith Shoesmith, Jack Underwood, Peter Bance, Albert Harding, William Baden Brown, Joseph Webb, Mr Rumins, Mr Booton, Geoffrey Long (with spectacles), -?-, Peter Booton. (*East Grinstead Observer*)

Latvians in the garden of Rowfant House, September 1974. A community has been living here since 1953. On the left is J. Kronbergs, one of the residents, with T. Pupurins, a London resident who at weekends helped maintain the house and garden. (*East Grinstead Observer*)

Seven

Schools, Sport and Entertainment

County (Grammar) School staff, dressed for stewarding and marshalling on Sports Day, 1935. From left to right, back row: Philip Sandall (geography), Harold Slatter (mathematics), Donald Bain (chemistry), Jimmy Evans (music), J.A. Royle (art), Tom W. Scott (French), W.J. Hollingsworth (woodwork). Front row: Miss K.E. Floyd (French), Miss M.M. Maudsley (domestic science), Richard L. Treble (headmaster 1928-1938), Miss N.H. Stapley (deputy head and history), Miss M.A Matthews (English), Miss R.E. Giddings (mathematics). (Harold Connold)

County (Grammar) School hockey team, 1932/33. From left to right, back row: Doris Divall, Vivien Wray, Winifred Butcher, Edna Wildish, Linda Clarke, Joan Sippetts. Front row: Jane Fox, Vera Smith, Kathleen Dixon (captain), Sybil Martin, Mattie Dunlop. (TM)

Imberhorne School pupils performing what is presumed to be a Passion Play in modern dress, 1960s. As so often happens, whoever took the picture failed to caption it and when the school donated it to the Town Museum in 1998 no one could be identified. (TM)

Imberhorne School sports stars, February 1977. From left to right: Alison Dawes, who was chosen to play for Sussex County Netball; Michelle Bass, who won the Sussex County Gymnastics; Gary Styles, who was chosen to play for the Sussex under-fifteens rugby; and Paul Dupoy, chosen to play rugby in a Sussex *v*. Bristol game. (*East Grinstead Observer*)

Imberhorne Middle School sports day, July 1977. Christine Mitchell takes the Long Jump in the Third Year Girls event. (*East Grinstead Observer*)

A cricket match in progress at the West Street ground, Whit Monday 26 May 1890. This was the opening day of the Cricket Club's new ground and probably the match shown was the first to be played there. The club secretary at that time was Robert Payne Crawfurd. (William Page)

Cricket pavilion on the West Street ground, 1900s. East Grinstead Cricket Club, founded in 1857, used the ground from 1890 and eleven years later this pavilion was built. Second and third from the right, back row, are believed to be Joseph Rice and his wife Sophia. (TM)

East Grinstead Post Office cricket team (front) *v.* East Grinstead Rugby Club team, 1966. From left to right, front row: Eric Styles Snr, Maurice Billings, Derek Penny, Ron Carter, Eric Styles Jnr, Ian Pesket, Mike Budgen, Maurice Furminger, Peter Gurney, -?-. Extreme right, back row: Hugh Macmillan, umpire. (*East Grinstead Courier*)

East Grinstead Rugby Football Club team at East Court, *c.* 1958. Back row, second from left: Don Bain (grammar school chemistry master); fifth, Twinn; tenth, Hutchings; eleventh, Brian Desmond, co-founder and secretary of the club and local journalist. Front row, first from left: Eddie Pitt; second, W.G.M. Fursdon, Grammar School woodwork master. (*East Grinstead Observer*)

Aerial view of Lingfield County Secondary School and its extensive grounds, looking north, *c.* 1958. First-year pupils were in the annexe, to the right of the straight footpath (twitten), while all others used the classrooms to the left. Behind the main buildings are 'prefab' classrooms of 1950 and, beyond them, the school garden. To the left of this are the playing field and tennis court; to its left is the school farm, beyond which are Vicarage Road and the Primary School. (Aerofilms, Boreham Wood)

Scene from James Bridie's play *Tobias and the Angel* at Lingfield County Secondary School, May 1959. This was the first school play that Leslie Laycock – head of English at Lingfield from 1957 to 1964 produced – careful attention was paid to music and effects, and it was a great success. Here, Gwen Whibley gives an impressive performance. (L.S. Laycock)

A touching scene from the Lingfield School presentation of *Tobias and the Angel*, May 1959. Derek Ridler played Tobias and Janis Pannell (extreme left) was the Angel. (L.S. Laycock)

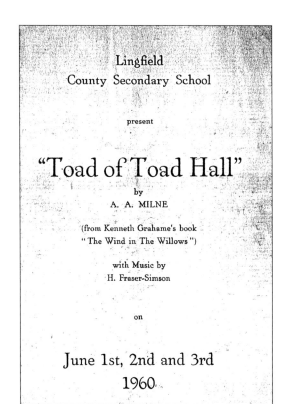

Lingfield
County Secondary School

present

"Toad of Toad Hall"

by
A. A. MILNE

(from Kenneth Grahame's book
"The Wind in The Willows")

with Music by
H. Fraser-Simson

on

June 1st, 2nd and 3rd
1960

An even more ambitious enterprise by Lingfield County Secondary School, 1960. This was the second play produced by Leslie Laycock, assisted by his wife Rita (who taught history). The entire cast of forty were pupils, and a further sixty children created the sets and costumes under staff direction, preparation taking many months of work. This play, like its predecessor, was a great success – deservedly so.

Four fourteen-year-old scholars, photographed by a classmate, of Form 3A, Lingfield County Secondary School, March 1961. They are positioned beneath the windows of the English and Maths classrooms. From left to right: Christopher Mayo, Derek Parkes, David Gould and John Winchester. (Michael Creasey)

Part of the former Lingfield County Secondary School, 30 June 1990. A 'Medieval Fair', with stallholders in costume, is in full swing in what was formerly the playground but latterly the staff car park. The left-hand gable contained the classroom in which the genial Leslie Laycock taught English; on the right was the mathematics room presided over by the formidable Fred McElvenny. (D. Gould)

Memorial plaque in a corridor close to the main entrance of Lingfield County Middle School – the former secondary school – June 1989. On 9 February 1943 at 8.30 a.m. a German bomb hit part of the school, killing two teachers, a cleaner and two eleven-year-old pupils who had arrived early. The school, which had opened in June 1907, was famed for its Farming Course, run by Austin Shorney from February 1948 to July 1970. Surrey County Council closed the school entirely in 1993. (D. Gould)

The Sackville Players' production of Shaw's *Arms and the Man* at East Grinstead Parish Hall, April 1959. It was directed by Louise Cuttell. From left to right: Maureen Yeates, Leslie Laycock (as Sergius), Roy Pegler (founder chairman of the Players) and Bernard Kempner. Leslie and Rita Laycock were leading lights in the Players from 1958 to 1964 and again from 1967, Leslie being chairman from 1968 to 1973. (*East Grinstead Courier*)

Eight of the cast of *All My Sons*, by Arthur Miller, which the Sackville Players presented at East Grinstead Parish Hall, November 1959. Leslie Laycock was the producer, and he and his wife also performed in it. From left to right, seated: Paddy Ellison, Eric Woodhatch, Christine Carpenter, Roy Pegler. Standing: Alan Newell, Violet Emy, Bernard Kempner, Allan Pegler. (*East Grinstead Courier*)

Handbill giving details of *All My Sons*, which the Sackville Players performed in November 1959. Their first play was put on in 1955 and five of their productions were co-winners in Sussex full-length Drama Festivals. Roy Pegler, the founder chairman, was succeeded by Leslie Laycock in 1968.

THE SACKVILLE PLAYERS

(President, Lady Sinderson)

present

ALL MY SONS

by ARTHUR MILLER

(New York Drama Critics' Award 1948)

at the

Parish Hall, East Grinstead

on **FRIDAY, NOVEMBER 20th** and
SATURDAY, NOVEMBER 21st, 1959
at 7.30 p.m.

Producer   LESLIE LAYCOCK

The cast includes :

Christine Carpenter	Paddy Ellison	Violet Emy
Bernard Kempner	Rita Laycock	Leslie Laycock
Allan Newell	Allan Pegler	Roy Pegler
	Eric Woodhatch	

Tickets available from The Wilmington Bookshop, 55/57 High St., East Grinstead — or from members of the cast, from Nov. 2nd.

Prices: 5/- numbered and reserved; 3/6, 2/6

Specially reduced prices for parties of six or more

PLEASE BOOK EARLY

Two members of the East Grinstead Operatic Society in a scene from *The Rebel Maid*, which was performed at the Whitehall Theatre in 1934. The society was formed in 1922, its staple fare being Gilbert and Sullivan operettas, though not exclusively. (Harold Connold)

Coronation Year

PROGRAMME

H.M.S. PINAFORE

EAST GRINSTEAD OPERATIC SOCIETY

Programme - - Sixpence

Cover of the programme for the Operatic Society's production of *HMS Pinafore*, November 1953. Typical of programmes printed by Cullen's in the 1950s, it gave full details of the cast, a description of the operetta's plot and, to defray costs, carried several advertisements of local businesses.

A group from *HMS Pinafore*, which the Operatic Society performed in November 1953. Seventh from left: Iris Milsom as Josephine; ninth, Kenneth Ormston as Ralph Rackstraw; eleventh, Walter Diplock as Dick Deadeye. Leslie Dungey took the role of Sir Joseph Porter. (Harold Connold)

Eight

The Railway

East Grinstead railway station, *c.* 1905. Opened on 1 August 1882, the station had a splendid main building designed by T.H. Myres of Preston. W.R. Pepper, in his *History and Guide* of 1885, wrote: 'The Station is a very commodious and convenient structure with handsome and spacious buildings. The drive up to the entrance is well arranged, a centre clump of plants, with lamp, forming a useful and pleasing object.' However, by 1971, British Rail considered it to be far too grandiose for a town of 21,000 inhabitants and demolished it, replacing it in 1972 with the present prefabricated structure. (William Page)

A Class E4 tank locomotive, having shunted its train from the up platform at East Grinstead Low Level, is entering the down platform, *c.* 1921. It will form the 3.7 p.m. to Haywards Heath. Porter signalman George 'Juggy' Wren, the picture of dignity, watches proceedings from the North signal cabin. (Kenneth Nutt)

Class I2 tank locomotive No. 19, built in July 1908, at the Low Level, c. 1921. It is standing beneath the bridge that carried the High Level station on the Three Bridges to Tunbridge Wells line – closed in January 1967. The engine is about to work an afternoon train to London. (Kenneth Nutt)

View from East Grinstead High Level station, looking east, *c.* 1905. On the left is Stenning's timber yard and on the right the Union Workhouse. In the distance are the goods yard and the disused station building of 1866, closed in October 1883 but not demolished until February 1908. (William Page)

London, Brighton & South Coast Railway Class E5 tank locomotive No. 567, built November 1902, at the London end of the Low Level station around 1921. Watched by porter signalman 'Juggy' Wren, the engine is approaching its train (out of shot) before departure for Oxted. (Kenneth Nutt)

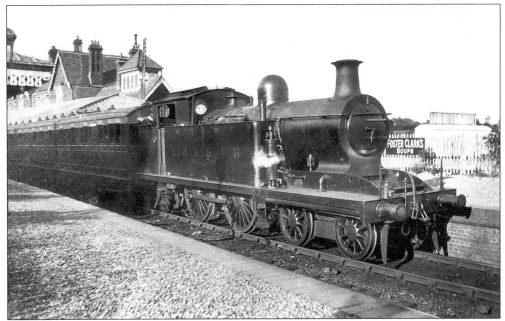

Class I1 tank locomotive No. 7, built in October 1907, at the Low Level, *c.* 1921. The train is formed of six-wheeled carriages and the only train on the Oxted line so-formed at this time was the 5.5 p.m. from Victoria, which after a half-hour wait at East Grinstead continued to Lewes at 7.7 p.m. (Kenneth Nutt)

A train in East Grinstead High Level station, 25 February 1921. The locomotive is one of the numerous Class D1 tank engines of the LB & SCR, No. 252, built by Neilson &º Co. of Glasgow in 1882. It is hauling Set Train No. 89, consisting of three bogie coaches, on a London to Tunbridge Wells service. (Kenneth Nutt)

EAST GRINSTEAD

(Sussex) from *Victoria* or *London Bridge*, via Dormans, 30 miles.
Map Square 23. Pop. 7,901.

Ordinary Single,
Victoria or London Bridge,
Via Dormans, 6/3a, 3/9c.
Via Three Bridges, 6/7a, 3/11c.
Summer Return,
Via Dormans, 8/6a, 5/0d.
Via Three Bridges, 9/0a, 5/3d.
Cheap Day (Note 6).
Via Dormans, 6/6a, 4/0c.
Via Three Bridges, 6/9a, 4/0c.
TICKET CONDITIONS, see page 1.

Leave Vict.	Lon. B.	Arr. at E. Grin.
A —	6.10h	7.27
M —	6.18h	7.48
6.30	—	7.51
—	7.20h	8.45
—	8. 3	9.23
9. 5*	—	10.25
10.19h	—	11.41
—	10.45	12. 2
P 12. 3 M	—	1.17
—	12. 5eh	1.22
—	12.16eh	1.47
—	12.30dh	1.47
—	12.47d	1.59
1.25d	—	2.23
—	1.33e*	2.55
1.32dh	—	2.55
—	1.38d*	2.56
2.46h	3. 0h	4. 1
4. 5dh	4. 9e	5.19
—	—	5.18
4.50 *	4.14d	5.25
—	—	6. 4
—	5. 0dh	6. 9
5.10	5. 9eh	6. 9
—	—	6.23
5.50	5.40e	6.50
—	—	7. 0
—	6.16dh	7.58
—	6.30e	7.44
—	6.40eh	7.58
6.48e	—	8. 8
6.53d	—	8. 8
—	7.40	8.55
7.46h	8. 0h	9. 7
9.14	—	10.30
10.30v	—	11.47
11.50x	—	1. 0

Sunday Trains.

Leave Vict.	Lon. B.	Arr. at E. Grin.
A —	8.35	9.48
M 10.15	—	11.33
P 6.28h	6.16h	7.37
M —	6.40	8. 3
7.46h	—	9. 4

Trains from East Grinstead.

Leave E. Grin.	Arrive at Lon. B.	Vict.
A 6.36h	—	8. 7
M 6.39	7.43	—
7. 9*	8.21	—
7.54	9. 0	—
7.58h	9. 8	—
8.12*	9.28	—
8.32	—	9.37
9. 7	10. 8	—
9.24h	10.20	—
9.32	10.39	—
10.30	—	11.41
10.33h	11.58	—
P 12. 6h	—	1.17
M 12.22	—	1.37
1.52	3. 4	—
1.55h	2.56	—
3.16h	4.34	—
3.38d	—	4.46
4.10	5.19	—

EAST GRINSTEAD—continued.

Leave E. Grin.	Arrive at Lon. B.	Vict.
P 4.15h	5.38	—
M 5. 7*	—	6.40
5.28h	6.56	—
6.22*	8. 6	—
7. 5	—	8.15
8. 9e	9.22	—
9.15	10.23	—
10.46	11.55	12. 5

Sunday Trains.

Leave E. Grin.	Arrive at Lon. B.	Vict.
A 8. 2h	—	9.12
M 9.56	—	11. 9
11.49	—	12.57
P 6.19h	7.35	—
M 8.11	9.28	—

d Saturdays only.
e Saturdays excepted.
h Via Three Bridges.
v 2nd and 4th Wednesdays only.
x 1st and 3rd Wednesdays only.

Taxi Cabs can be hired to meet any train at this station by telegram, or telephone No. 13, to NUTT, Station Road, East Grinstead.

Ye Felbridge Hotel. An Ideal old-world Residential and Motorists' Hotel. See advt. p. 156.

Ye Dorset Arms Hotel. Established over 300 years. First class for Military, Families and Motorists. Main Eastbourne and Brighton roads. Hot Luncheons and Table d'Hôte daily. Officially appointed A.A. and R.A.C. Best centre for beauty spots of Sussex and Surrey. Telephone No. 24.

Crown Hotel. Family and Commercial. Most centrally situated. Comfortable Commercial Dining and Sitting Rooms. Ordinary daily, 1 o'clock. Motors. Posting. Garage. Good Stabling. Billiards. Telephone 117. Prop., STANLEY C. BALL.

Train service to and from London and East Grinstead, summer 1934. All through trains via Dormans are shown; on those marked with an asterisk passengers changed at Oxted and the 10.46 p.m. from East Grinstead terminated at East Croydon. Passengers travelling via Three Bridges had to change there, except on the 4.5 and 5.9 p.m. from London, which were through-trains.

Class M7 tank locomotive No. 30055 on a two-coach train from Three Bridges to East Grinstead near Imberhorne Lane, c. 1960. This engine was built by the London & South Western Railway in 1905 and was based at Three Bridges depot from late 1959 to early 1962; it was withdrawn from service in September 1963. (Norman Sherry)

Type '3' diesel-electric locomotive and three-coach train at the High Level, working the 6.25 a.m. from Victoria to Tunbridge Wells West, 1963. On the right is the cutting in which ran the line to the Low Level station, and behind are the houses in Grosvenor Road. The locomotive is in its original dark green livery with cream band. (Norman Sherry)

East Grinstead High Level station water crane, at the west-end of the northernmost island platform, 1960. Looking up at the tank, which was installed in around 1920, are the photographer's daughters Annette Elizabeth (left) and Meryl Anne Sherry (right). (Norman Sherry)

St Clair bridge, Dormans Park, being blown up, July 1977. This bridge stood a quarter of a mile south of Dormans station. The picture was taken immediately after the moment of detonation and the structure is just about to collapse. (*East Grinstead Observer*)

Class 33 diesel-electric locomotive No. 33027, *Earl Mountbatten of Burma*, at East Grinstead station about to leave with the 17.04 to London Bridge, 14 April 1981. One of a very few of the class to have received a name, it is in British Rail blue livery with white cab roofs. The 'Cromptons' regularly worked certain peak-hour trains between 1963 and l986. (D. Gould)

Derailed locomotive at East Grinstead, 22 August 1981. The line between here and Oxted had been closed for track renewal and this 'Crompton', working a northbound engineers' train, had run off the trap points at the platform end. A steam-worked breakdown crane re-railed the locomotive by midday. *(East Grinstead Courier)*

Cooks Pond viaduct, looking south, May 1988. While the bridge was being built the pond was drained, but after the line was opened (10 March 1884) the pond refilled. W.R. Pepper in 1885 wrote: 'This viaduct is so light a structure that it seems utterly unfit to bear the weight of passing trains'. There are five wrought-iron lattice girder spans. (D. Gould)

Dormans station entrance, c. 1925. The station, opened on 10 March 1884, was intended to serve the Bellaggio Estate – later named Dormans Park – rather than the village of Dormansland, to which it is connected by footpath. Although the building has changed little some one hundred years later, it is now sadly neglected thanks to de-staffing.

Nine

Buses

East Grinstead High Street looking east, showing a London Transport 'T' type single-deck bus No. T649 on service 434, June 1947. This route normally ran between Edenbridge and Horsham via Dormansland, East Grinstead, Crawley Down, Three Bridges and Crawley, but the bus in the picture appears to be on an extra, short working, terminating at East Grinstead. The regular bus is right behind it. (Harold Connold)

East Grinstead Motor Coaches Gilford CP 6 of 1929 in Cantelupe Road, *c.* 1937. The vehicle was acquired second hand in 1936 and disposed of two years later. Driver Horace Richard Medhurst (1911-1986) started with the company in September 1931 as a conductor, progressing to driver in 1932 and finally inspector, devising duty sheets and special traffic arrangements.

Advertisement from *East Grinstead – the Official Guide*, 1948. East Grinstead Motor Coaches became a limited company named Sargent's of East Grinstead in summer 1948, operating private-hire coaches and stage-carriage services. The three bus routes were: East Grinstead-Cowden, East Grinstead-Ashurst Wood and Edenbridge-Crowborough. The company gave up its bus services in March 1951.

Frank Cooper and his 'Pioneer' bus outside Grassmere, Forest View Road, early 1920s. He was the first bus operator to run a through service between East Grinstead and Tunbridge Wells (November 1923 to January 1926); but he could not compete with East Surrey Traction Co. and in 1930 he sold his charabanc business to East Grinstead Coaches.

Contretemps between bus and lorry in the narrow College Lane, 19 October 1971. One of Hall & Co.'s lorries seems to be well stuck as London Country Bus Services 'Swift' No. SM 145 on route 434 from Edenbridge to Horsham squeezes past. (*East Grinstead Observer*)

Two London Country Bus Services employees pose outside Garland Road bus garage, East Grinstead, December 1981. This was shortly before its closure and their retirement. Left: Jock Ritson, depot inspector; right : Don Banks, traffic superintendent. (*East Grinstead Courier*)

An aspect of bus operation the public does not see: checking a ticket machine against a waybill, Garland Road, December 1981. Claude Ellis, a depot inspector, started work at this garage in 1946 and retired on 31 December 1981, the day it closed. (*East Grinstead Courier*)

London Country Bus Services No. XF 3 at Baldwins Hill, 2 May 1981. Of the eight experimental Fleetline double-deck buses that were introduced in 1965, by 1981 this was the only one in regular use. Here it is on route 475 working the 9.17 from Dormansland to East Grinstead via Lingfield. (D. Gould)

Experimental Fleetline No. XF 3 now at Dormansland, 2 May 1981. Route 485 operated between East Grinstead and Dormansland via Queen Victoria Hospital, certain journeys being extended to Edenbridge and Westerham. Here the 14.43 East Grinstead-Dormansland is in the High Street at the junction with Hollow Lane. (D. Gould)

Leyland National bus No. SNB 132 operates the final 21.13 journey on route 424 from East Grinstead to Reigate, 31 December 1981. On its return from Reigate this was the last bus in traffic to enter Garland Road garage; there were eighteen passengers. Driver Jim Bishop poses with bus enthusiasts Ken Robinson, Keith Mason and Richard Godfrey. (*East Grinstead Courier*)

Driver/operator Jim Bishop at the wheel of Leyland National bus No. SNB 132, the last to be operated from East Grinstead garage on the evening of 31 December 1981. Many of the staff retired, while others had to transfer to Crawley or Godstone garages. (*East Grinstead Courier*)

Maidstone & District Motor Services bus No. 3463 of 1973 at Forest Row, Good Friday 1984. It is on service 291 working the 14.40 East Grinstead to Tunbridge Wells. A very long-established route, it was numbered 91 until around 1974. Outside the post office stands an iron 'Bow Bells' milepost showing 33 miles from Cornhill, London. (D. Gould)

Bizarre sight on a Southdown Motor Services bus in East Grinstead in the week before Christmas 1980. Santa Claus, it seems, has forsaken his normal mode of transport but the three young passengers are unperturbed. From left to right: Paul Goodall, Francois Bonin, Mark Holman, driver Tony Elms. (*East Grinstead Observer*)

Chelwood Common Pillar Box, 9 July 1983. A Southdown bus on service 170, working the 10.57 East Grinstead to Haywards Heath, is hotly pursued by another on service 780 working the 11.00 East Grinstead to Eastbourne. Service 170 was renumbered 770 on 3 March 1986 and withdrawn on 24 October 1987, Southdown's last route to serve East Grinstead. (D. Gould)

Turners Hill, The Crown, 11 July 1983. London Country Bus Services Leyland National No. SNB 334 pauses to take a passenger while working service 434, the 14.39 East Grinstead to Crawley. The large tree outside The Crown was a victim of the great storm of 1987. (D. Gould)

Ten
Horse Transport

A splendid line-up of Hall & Co.'s carts in Chequer Road, East Grinstead, c. 1910. From around 1899 Hall & Co., coal, lime and slate merchants – whose headquarters were in Croydon – had their East Grinstead depot at No. 116 London Road at the entrance to the High Level station goods yard. From left to right are carts Nos 151, 47, 101 and 175. (TM)

'Four-horse power', the title given by the photographer, 1930s. Although location and date are unknown, this picture of a timber dray by East Grinstead's professional photographer from 1926 to 1959 is included as an example of his most pleasing work. Even the Austin motor car is no clue to the location as it bears a London registration. (Harold Connold)

Nutt Bros. stableyard, Station Road, c. 1920. Jack Pentecost is driving a French victoria, a conveyance that would have greeted passengers coming off the trains for (by an agreement dated 16 March 1906) Messrs Stone & Nutt had the exclusive privilege to ply with cabs, broughams and other carriages in the station forecourt, the railway receiving £2 10s per quarter. (Kenneth Nutt)

Horse-drawn farm cart in the High Street, East Grinstead, 4 May 1981. Forming part of the attractions on a damp May Fair Day it is passing opposite the Rose and Crown. (D. Gould)

One of Laurie and Val Taylor's horse-drawn conveyances making a special appearance in East Grinstead High Street on May Fair Day, 4 May 1981. The first of these annual events was in 1979, the High Street being closed to normal traffic for most of the day. (D. Gould)

A surprising sight in the 1980s: a two horse carriage setting off from Brickhouse Farm, Horne, July 1984. Laurie and Val Taylor, who at the time owned seventeen vintage carriages, many of which had required extensive restoration, were both members of Windsor Park Equestrian Club. (*East Grinstead Courier*)

Farm cart outside the Hay Waggon Inn, Hartfield, January 1982. For many years this was a Hartfield landmark but unfortunately the vehicle's deteriorating condition resulted in its removal a few years ago. (D. Gould)

Eleven
Road Motor Vehicles

Shell lorry No. 3764 on solid tyres in Station Road, East Grinstead, early 1920s. At that time Shell had a depot adjoining the yard of William Best & Son, coal merchants. This lorry was an early type of petrol tanker; cranking the engine is Alf Barton (who later worked for Nutt's Garage) and with him is 'Lorry Boy' Payne. (Kenneth Nutt)

A Standard Motor Co. 11.6 of 1922 at Nutt Bros. garage, Station Road, 1920s. In the centre is foreman driver Bert Buddle and, right, William Gilder ('Old Tot'), one of Nutt's horse-cab drivers, who fought in the Afghan War. (Kenneth Nutt)

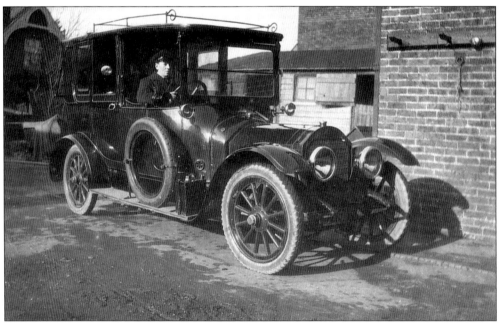

Nutt Bros. Unic taxi of 1913 at Station Road, c. 1920. This 'Three quarter Landaulette' was bought second hand from Unic agents Mann & Overton of Battersea Bridge Road and later fitted with electric lamps. Its driver here is Walter Payne. At this time Nutt Bros. owned four taxis, all Unics, two having been bought new and the others second hand. (Kenneth Nutt)

Nutt Bros. Ford taxi at Station Road, 11 July 1921. This vehicle, new in 1921, had left-hand drive but an English-made body. The driver, one of Nutt's employees, is Douglas Hunt, who later left to join East Surrey Traction Co. (Kenneth Nutt)

A Renault of 1910 at Nutt Bros. garage, Station Road, 1920s. Its owner was Douglas Newbold of Imberley Lodge, off Coombe Hill Road. Nutt's employee Bert Buddle is washing the car. (Kenneth Nutt)

A very rare car: a Chater-Lea, *c.* 1921. Nutt's would charge a motorist 1s for leaving his car in their yard for a day. Posing for the photographer is George Leppard at the wheel and, beside him, William Gilder (Old Tot). On the right is a brougham. (Kenneth Nutt)

Another of Nutt Bros. taxis – an ex-Army Ford, *Ole Liz*, 12 July 1921. It was bought second hand from the North Sussex Garage, London Road. The driver is Jim Leppard (the brother of George), a cheery and friendly fellow who died in March 1936 after thirty-one years' service with Nutt's. (Kenneth Nutt)

Bedford appliance of East Sussex Fire Brigade at East Grinstead fire station, 29 September 1973. The town's youngsters appear to have commandeered the machine, but during the annual open day of the station such scenes were to be expected. The vehicle was registered in East Sussex in 1966. (*East Grinstead Observer*)

Stanley Budgen, of Copthorne, with his restored fire engine, June 1979. Formerly with Seaford Urban District Council Fire Brigade, this appliance was registered in 1939. Stan would often display it at fire station open days. (*East Grinstead Observer*)

Chevrolet motor lorry of C. & H. Gasson Ltd, *c*. 1930. This firm was in business at No. 153 London Road, East Grinstead, from 1894 to 1980; originally smiths and wheelwrights, then brick and tile makers, builders and contractors, from the mid-1920s they became builders' merchants. This picture was taken by the driver of the lorry. (G.E. Leppard)

A road roller, built by John Fowler & Co. (Leeds) Ltd, passing through East Grinstead High Street, September 1949. This machine was registered in West Sussex in the early 1930s. The building with the round-headed windows on the first floor was used by the Sisterhood of St Margaret from 1858 to 1870, when they moved into their new convent. (N.H. Pearson)

William Best & Son's steam tractor, built by William Foster & Co. Ltd at Lincoln around 1909, passing North End, East Grinstead, 1913. It is hauling two trailers containing children on a St Mary's church Sunday School outing to Blindley Heath common. Named *Wellington*, the tractor was normally used for conveying coal, but Best had obtained a hackney licence that allowed him to carry passengers. He disposed of the tractor around 1932. (William Page)

A steamroller at work at the bottom of Blackwell Road and Blackwell Hollow, September 1949. Built by Aveling & Porter Ltd of Rochester and registered in Surrey in 1928, this roller was owned by A.J. Ward & Son of Egham. To the right of the machine is seen the former Blackwell Farm house. (N.H. Pearson)

A Wallis & Steevens Ltd 'Advance' steamroller working on new road construction, Woods Hill Close, Ashurst Wood, c. 1961. This machine was built at Basingstoke around 1927-1928 and its owner and driver here is Frank Greasley. (N.H. Pearson)

Twelve
Where Are We?

A cast-iron signpost at Saint Hill Green, *c.* 1910. This shows that we are 1½ miles from East Grinstead, 11 miles from Godstone and 31½ miles from London. Behind the post is seen part of Saint Hill Farmhouse, which was built in the 1860s. (TM)

Forest Row village sign just unveiled, 1971. Despite the poor weather conditions the parish councillors look pleased with their new sign, which was made by Ken and John Grantham, the Ashurst Wood blacksmiths. (*East Grinstead Observer*)

Forest Row, winner of the best kept large village in East Sussex, November 1975. The sign was erected on the green in front of the village hall. From left to right: Ken Lang, Peter Griffits, Ruth Norcliffe and Alison MacPherson. Forest Row retained the plaque for one year. (*East Grinstead Observer*)

Ashurst Wood's new village sign, 28 November 1974. Members of the Women's Institute gather round the sign, which was made by Ken and John Grantham and their assistant Eric Lamprell. Front row, from left: fourth Jo Parkinson, fifth Pam Miller-Richards, sixth Jean Lewin. (*East Grinstead Observer*)

Milepost near Wych Cross showing distance from Cornhill, London April 1984. Made of cast iron, the post incorporates a stylised honeysuckle design above the numerals and a foliated patera below. It was erected around 1825 by the Godstone to Highgate Turnpike Trust, whose other mileposts (late eighteenth century) were of the 'Bow Bells' type. (D. Gould)

Wooden direction sign at the junction of Imberhorne Lane with London Road, East Grinstead, *c.* 1970. It was constructed by an Urban District Council craftsman and, though it has since been replaced, other similar posts may still be found in East Sussex. (East Grinstead Urban District Council photograph)